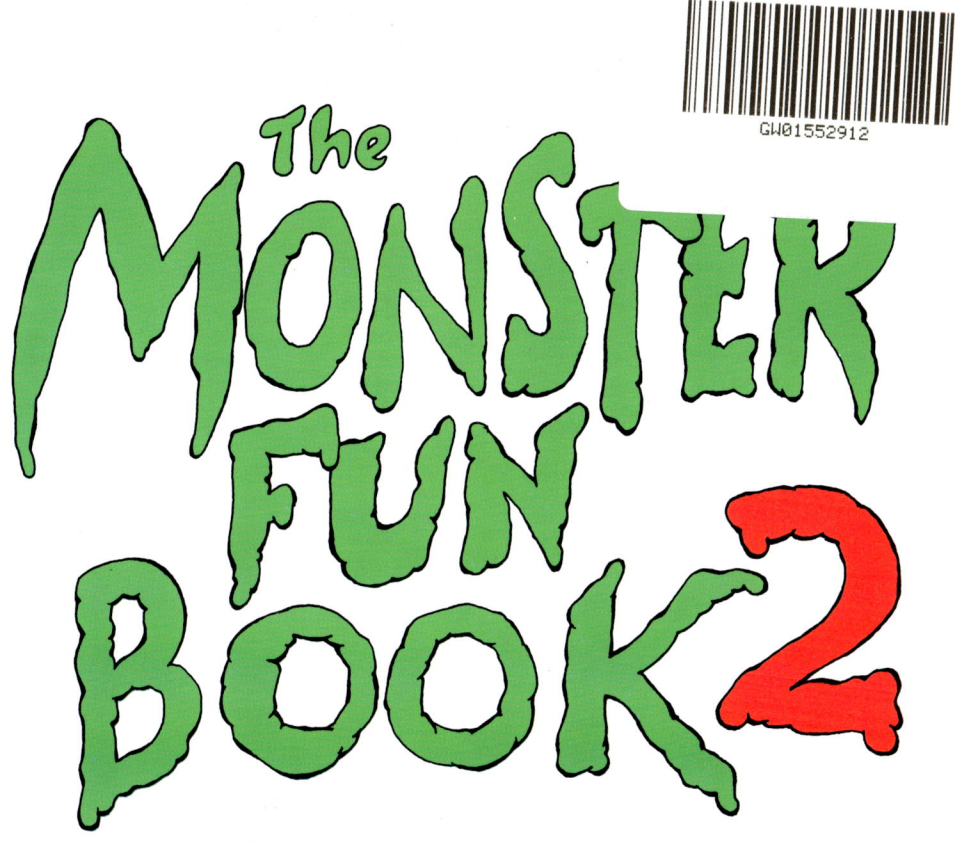

The Monster Fun Book 2

Steve Smallman

Scholastic Children's Books,
Scholastic Publications Ltd,
7-9 Pratt Street, London NW1 0AE, UK

Scholastic Inc.,
555 Broadway, New York, NY10012-3999, USA

Scholastic Canada Ltd,
123 Newkirk Road, Richmond Hill,
Ontario, Canada L4C 3G5

Ashton Scholastic Pty Ltd,
P O Box 579, Gosford, New South Wales,
Australia

Ashton Scholastic Ltd,
Private Bag 92801, Penrose, Auckland,
New Zealand

First published in the UK by Scholastic Publications Ltd, 1994

Copyright © Steve Smallman, 1994

ISBN 0 590 55498 0

Printed in Hong Kong by Paramount Printing Group

10 9 8 7 6 5 4 3 2 1

All rights reserved

The right of Steve Smallman to be identified as the author and illustrator of this work has been asserted by him in accordance with the Copyright, Designs and Patents Act, 1988.

This book is sold subject to the condition that it shall not, by way of trade or otherwise be lent, resold, hired out, or otherwise circulated without the publisher's prior consent in any form of binding or cover other than that in which it is published and without a similar condition, including this condition, being imposed upon the subsequent purchaser.

Friendly Monsters

Monsters don't have to be scary, they can be absolutely adorable like this little selection.

MONSTER MAKING INSTRUCTIONS

Ask an adult to help you make the slots and other tricky bits. Score by pushing a blunt pencil or the edge of a ruler along the dotted lines. This will make folding easier.

THE FLUBGUZZLER (CARD 1)

- Carefully pull out card 1 from the middle of the book.
- Cut out all the Flubguzzler pieces, cut the slots, and score along the dotted lines. Cut around the teeth (but not the gums) and cut out the eye-holes.
- Attach tongue tab D to slot D.
- Ask for help to make holes K.
- Push a split pin through holes K, fix piece J behind the eye-holes then bend back flaps E to secure. Add whiskers H and I.
- Now fold along the dotted lines A, B and C to create the mouth. (Bend the teeth slightly forward so that they interlock when mouth is shut.) Bend back flaps F and G.
- Holding the Flubguzzler by the back of his mouth, use ring J to move his eyes and tab D to move his tongue.

And now here's lunch...

THE FLUB (CARD 1)

- Carefully cut out all the Flub pieces, cut the slots, cut along the line of the mouth, and score along the dotted lines.
- Insert tab A into slot A to make the body.
- Push tongue B through slot B then out again through the mouth. Add hands C and spike D.

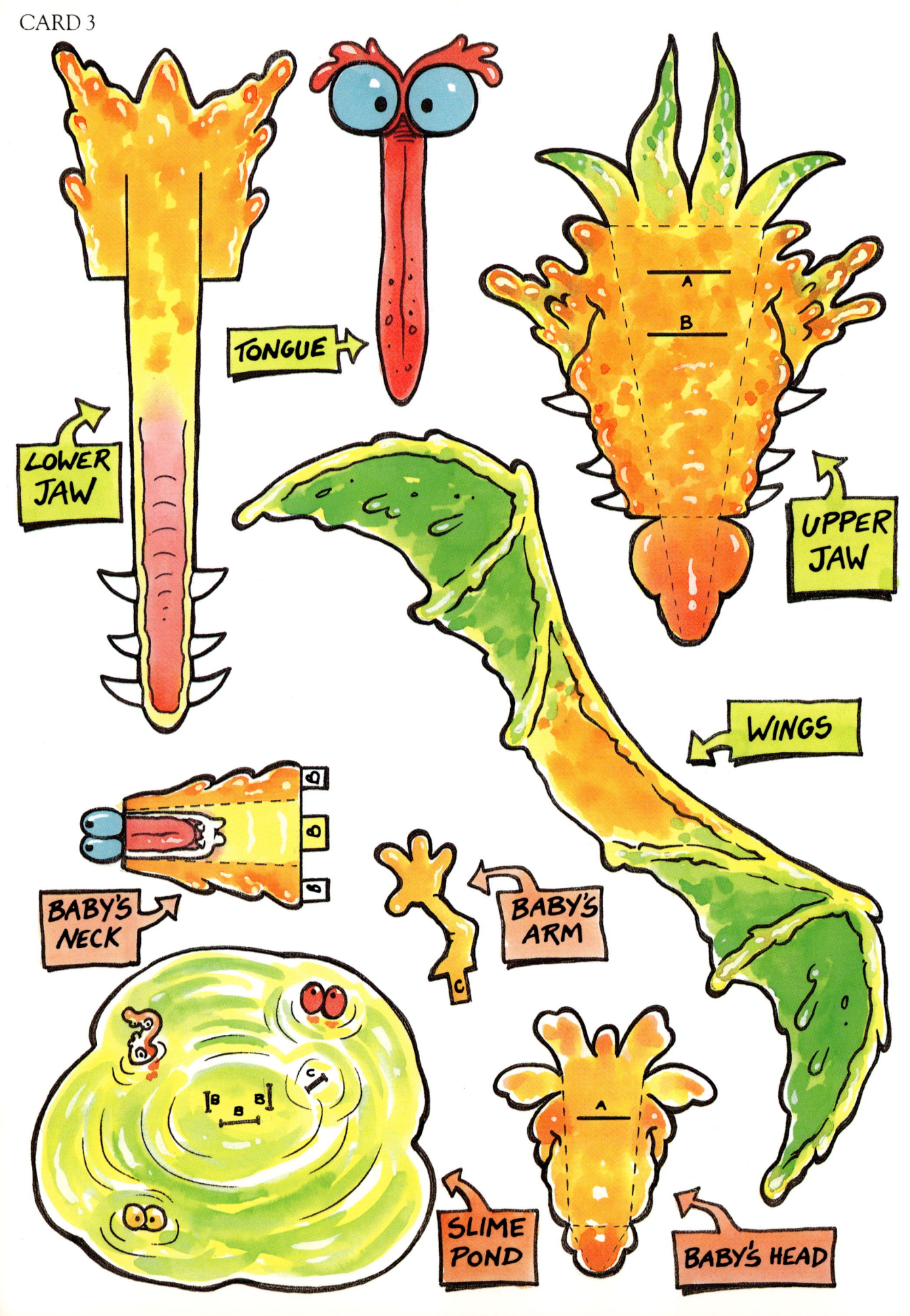

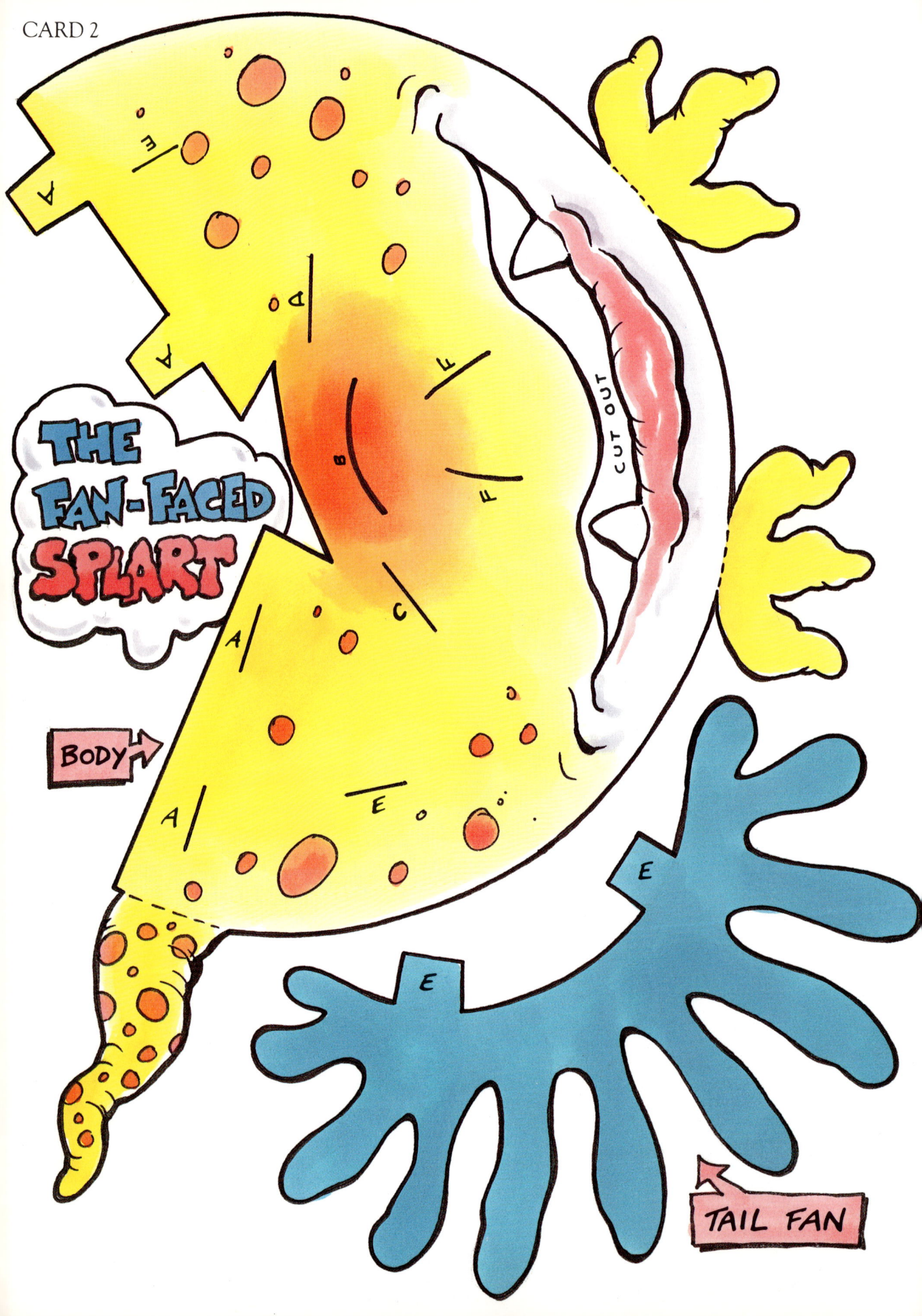

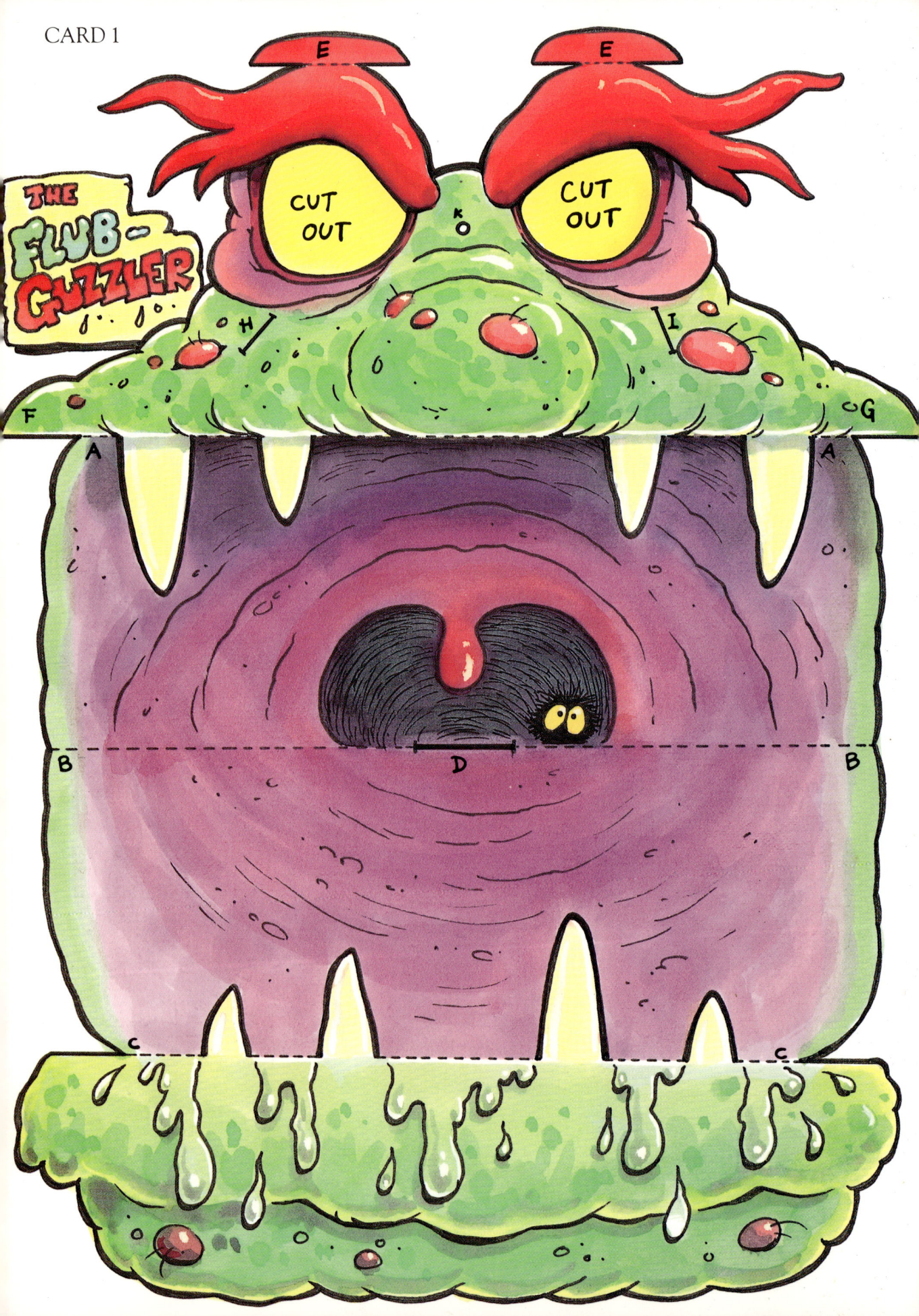

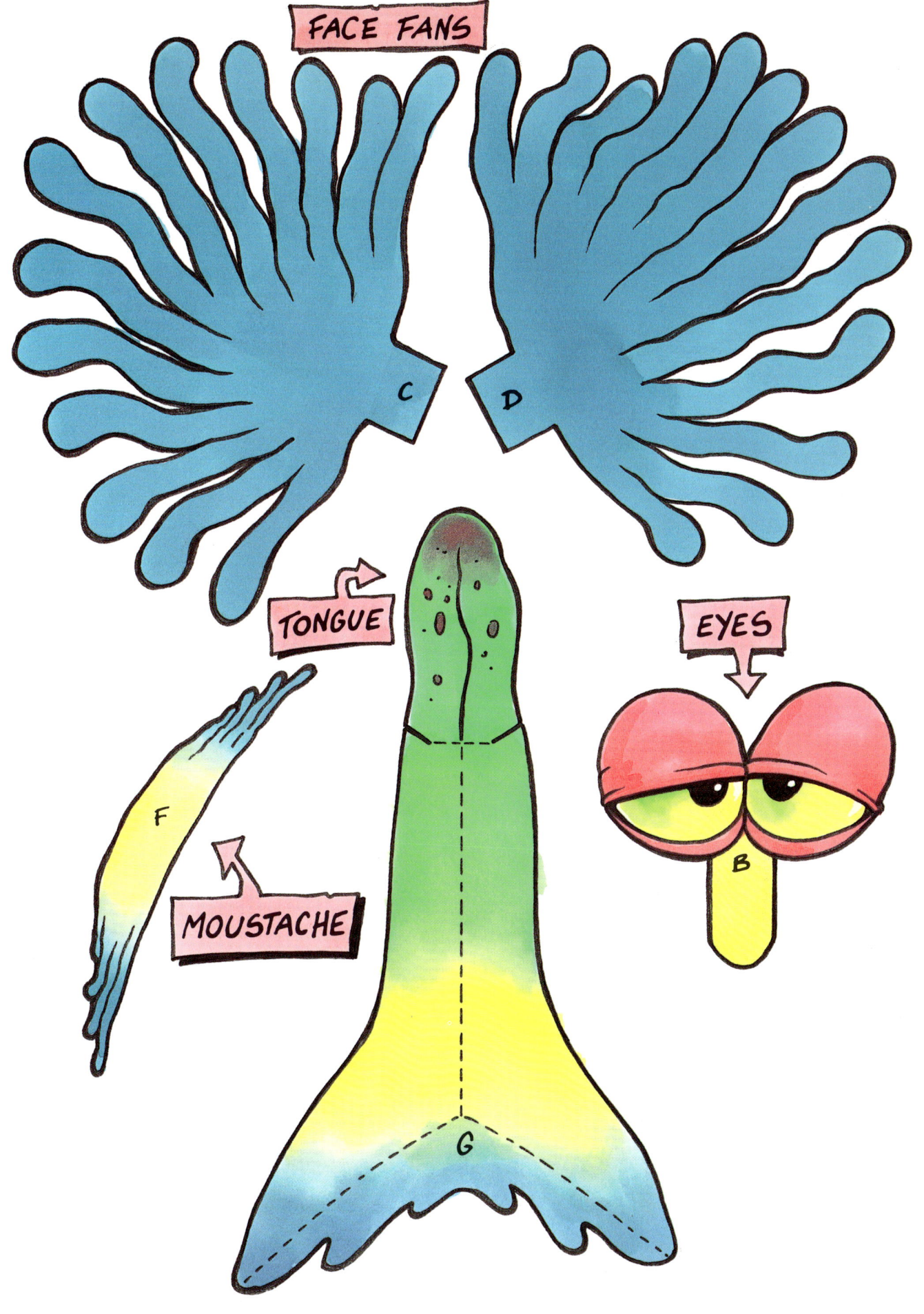

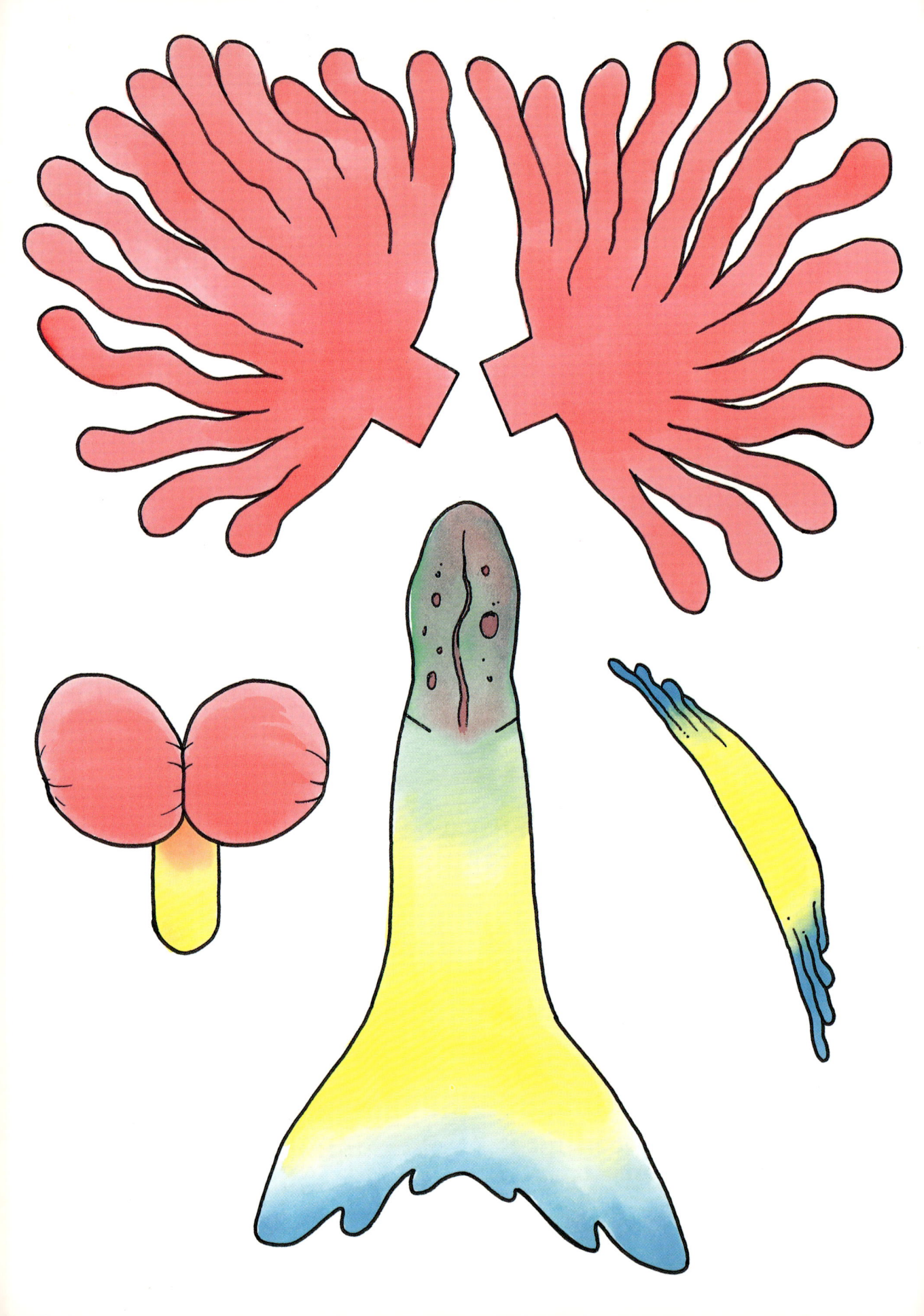

THE FAN-FACED SPLART (CARD 2)

- Carefully pull out card 2 from the middle of the book.
- Cut out all the pieces, cut the slots, score along the dotted lines, and cut out the mouth.
- Insert tabs A into slots A to make the body.
- Fold the tongue section along the dotted lines and push (tongue end first) into the triangular hole at the top of the body, then pull the tongue out of the mouth.
- Add eyes through slot B, fans and moustaches through slots C, D, E and F.
- Push flap G in and out to move the tongue.

THE SLIME-DRAGONS OF NARG (CARD 3)

- Carefully pull card 3 from the middle of the book.
- Cut out all the pieces, cut the slots, and score along the dotted lines.

FOR THE MOTHER SLIME DRAGON...

- **The Head** Fold in the teeth of the lower jaw then push it from underneath the upper jaw through slot A as far as it will go. Fold the horns along the dotted line and push them through the space between A and B, then push the lower jaw back through slot B to secure the horns in place.
- Insert the eyes and tongue through slot B.
- **The Body** Fold along dotted lines C, D and E and insert tab F into slot F.
- Slide the wings through slots G, then bend the tail into the shape you want.
- Push tab AA on the neck up through slot A on the head to join the head and body together.

AND HER BABY SLIME-DRAGON...

- Push the eyes up through slot A in the head.
- Fold along dotted lines on neck to shape neck.
- Insert neck B into slime pond, and flatten underneath.
- Insert arm C into slime pond, and flatten underneath.
- Fold along dotted lines on head to shape head.

EDIBLE MUD MONSTERS

These chocolate-coated Mud Monster cakes are easy to make and delicious to eat!

You will need:
6 small sponge cakes
1 200g (7oz) bar of cooking chocolate
1 packet of ready-roll icing
chocolate drops
white chocolate buttons
red food colouring
1 cocktail stick

(1) Put the sponge cakes upside-down on a baking sheet.

(2) Break the chocolate into pieces and ask for help to melt it in a bowl placed over a pan of boiling water.

(3) Roll some of the icing into 12 small balls (approx. 1cm in diameter).

(4) One by one, spear the balls with a cocktail stick and dip them halfway into the melted chocolate.

(5) Pour the remaining chocolate over the cakes till they are completely covered and the chocolate starts to pool at the base.

(6) Stick the balls white side forward onto the top of each cake and then leave them to set.

(7) With a sharp knife cut a mouth in the chocolate. Then cut the white chocolate buttons in half to make teeth and push them into the mouth.

(8) Mix a drop of red food colouring with some of the icing and use it to make tongues.

(9) Place the tongues into the mouth so that they hang down to the base.

(10) Finally, push chocolate drops into the holes left by the cocktail stick in the eyes.

(11) GOBBLE THEM UP!

With just a few small changes to the eyes, eyebrows and mouth you can show a whole range of expressions:
PRACTISE drawing just eyes and mouths to see how many different emotions you can create!

Then use whichever expression you want on the monster of your choice.

ADD SOME SWEAT TO MAKE HIM LOOK EVEN MORE NERVOUS!

A BIG NOSE MAY COVER PART OF THE MOUTH - JUST CONTINUE IT ON THE OTHER SIDE.

YOU CAN TRY PUTTING THE EYEBROWS IN MID-AIR!

A BIG DROOLING TONGUE MAKES HIM LOOK HUNGRY!

'WOBBLE' LINES SUGGEST SHAKING WITH FEAR.

A LITTLE CRESCENT SHADOW SUGGESTS A BOTTOM LIP.

TURN OVER TO HAVE A GO!

OPEN MOUTHS CAN BE EFFECTIVE

HAPPY   SCARED/SAD

ALTHOUGH THE LINE OF THIS MOUTH GOES UP AND DOWN IT'S THE LAST LITTLE BIT THAT SHOWS THE EXPRESSION - A = HAPPY, B = GRUMPY!

BLANK FACES

These monsters all look pretty blank! Can you draw their expressions using page 17 to help you?

- HUNGRY
- WORRIED (OPEN-MOUTHED)
- BLISSFULL
- SURPRISED
- SAD

(3)

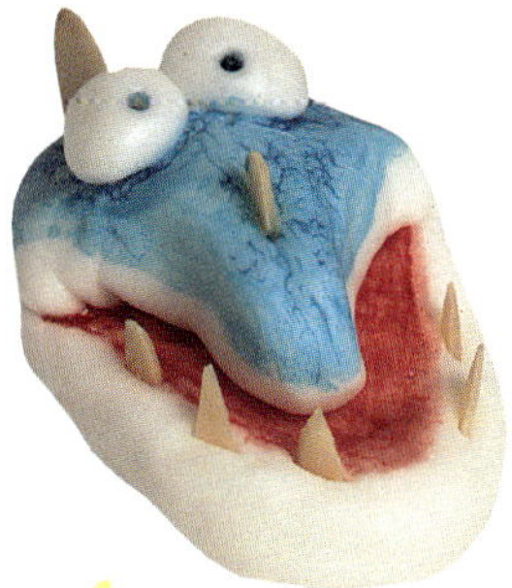

MAKE A LONG TAPERED 'SAUSAGE' SHAPE

FOLD THE 'SAUSAGE' IN HALF

ADD FLAKED ALMOND TEETH, HORNS AND SPIKES

ADD EYEBALLS.

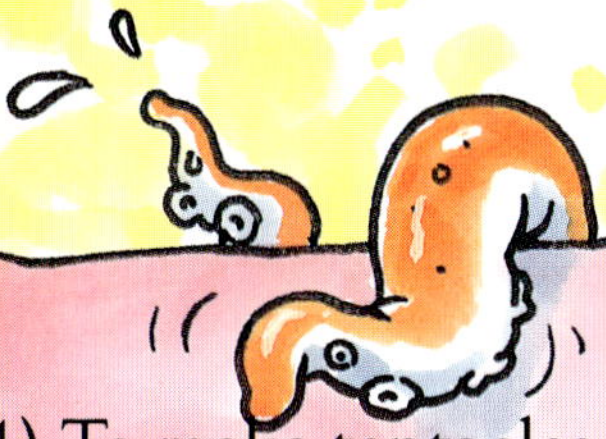

(4) To make tentacles: roll carrot shapes from the ready-roll icing. Then roll several small balls of icing to make the suckers. Place the balls on one side of the carrots then poke a cocktail stick through each ball. Now bend each tentacle into an S shape.

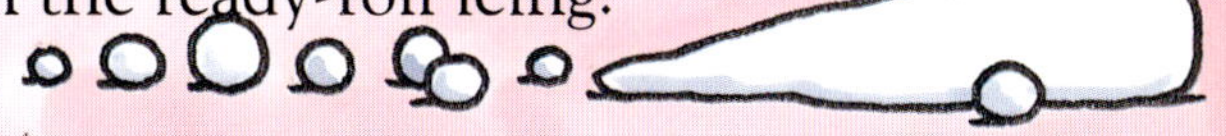

(5) Pour the 2 types of jelly into a shallow dish and stir lightly to make your swamp. Leave to set.

(6) Paint your swamp creatures with food colourings. Then add them to your swamp and serve!

23